Presidio House

# Rolo Slang for Brave Foreigners

Bogota Edition

Presidio House LLC
2026

ISBN-13: 979-8-9951420-2-7

Disclaimer

This book is a non-fiction educational and cultural guide to authentic colloquial Colombian Spanish. It contains real slang expressions used in everyday speech across different regions of Colombia, including informal, vulgar, strong, or regionally specific language that may be considered offensive, crude, or inappropriate in formal settings. All content is presented solely for linguistic, cultural, and educational purposes to help readers understand and communicate more naturally with native speakers.

The author and publisher do not endorse or encourage the use of profane, vulgar, or disrespectful language. Reader discretion is advised, especially for younger audiences or in professional/educational environments.

---

## Welcome from La Vecina

¡Bienvenido al mundo rolo, mijo! Soy la Vecina de Bogotá — la que te saluda con un "buenos días" aunque sean las tres de la tarde, pero te dice las verdades sin anestesia y con una media sonrisa. Aquí el tono es más seco, más irónico, más "tranqui pero pilas". Tú vas a aprender a saludar sin tanto alboroto, a aprobar con clase y a no dar papaya en la ciudad que nunca duerme. Esto es Bogotá puro, sin vueltas ni cuentos. Bienvenido a la capital.

## English Welcome

Welcome to the Rolo World, friend! I'm your Bogotá Vecina — the one who greets you with "good morning" even at 3 p.m., but tells you the truth without sugar-coating and with a slight smirk. The vibe here is drier, more ironic, more "chill but alert." You're going to learn how to greet without too much noise, approve with style, and never give papaya in the city that never sleeps. This is pure Bogotá — no fluff, no drama. Welcome to the capital.

---

## How to Use This Book

Each entry is set up the same way so you can jump in without unnecessary drama:

Phrase – the exact Rolo slang expression you're going to use

Vecina – that's me breaking it down in my straight, no-nonsense Bogotá voice

Meaning – the clear English sense and the real vibe behind it

Example – a real-life sentence the way we actually say it in the capital

Translation – the natural English version so you catch the tone

Say them out loud with that dry rolo delivery. Slang here is all about timing and attitude — keep it tranqui but pilas. You've got this.

# Table of Contents

## Saludos Rolo sin Tanto Alboroto

Rolo Greetings Without the Drama

(Entries 1–10)

**Entry 1**

**¿Todo bien o qué?**

**Vecina:**

Tú sueltas esto y ya estás hablando como un rolo de verdad — seco, directo y con ese toque bogotano que no regala sonrisas de gratis.

**Meaning:** Straight Bogotá greeting meaning "all good or what?"

**Example:** ¿Todo bien o qué? Se te ve la cara de lunes eterno.

**Translation:** All good or what? You look like it's eternal Monday on your face.

**Entry 2**

**¿Qué más?**

**Vecina:**

Corto, seco y efectivo — el saludo rolo por excelencia. Tú lo usas y la gente te responde con una media sonrisa mientras sigue caminando bajo la lluvia.

**Meaning:**

Minimalist Bogotá greeting meaning “what’s up?”

**Example:**

¿Qué más? ¿Ya desayunaste o sigues en ayunas?

**Translation:**

What’s up? Have you eaten breakfast or are you still fasting?

---

**Entry 3**

**¿Todo tranqui?**

**Vecina:**

“Tranqui” es la palabra rola por excelencia — calma con un toque de sarcasmo sutil. Tú lo dices y ya estás chequeando si la vaina está bajo control.

**Meaning:**

Chill greeting meaning “everything calm / relaxed?”

**Example:**

¿Todo tranqui? Porque yo estoy que exploto del tráfico.

**Translation:**

Everything calm? Because I’m about to explode from the traffic.

---

**Entry 4**

**¿Cómo va?**

**Vecina:**

Simple, educado, pero con ese toque de "no me cuentes toda tu vida". Tú lo usas y la gente te responde sin alboroto, puro estilo capitalino.

**Meaning:**

Polite Bogotá check-in meaning "how's it going?"

**Example:**

¿Cómo va? No me diga que otra vez se quedó en TransMilenio.

**Translation:**

How's it going? Don't tell me you got stuck in TransMilenio again.

---

**Entry 5**

**¿Qué hubo?**

**Vecina:**

Clásico rolo, seco pero cálido a su manera. Tú lo sueltas y ya estás abriendo la puerta para que te cuenten lo que pasó sin tener que insistir.

**Meaning:**

Casual Bogotá greeting meaning "what's up / what happened?"

**Example:** ¿Qué hubo? ¿Ya llegó el pedido o seguimos esperando?

**Translation:**

What's up? Did the delivery arrive or are we still waiting?

---

**Entry 6**

**¿Todo en orden?**

**Vecina:**

Formalito pero irónico, típico de Bogotá. Tú lo preguntas y la gente sabe que estás medio bromeando porque aquí casi nada está realmente en orden.

**Meaning:**

Slightly formal check meaning "everything in order?"

**Example:**

¿Todo en orden? Porque yo estoy en desorden total.

**Translation:**

Everything in order? Because I'm in total chaos.

---

**Entry 7**

**¿Qué tal?**

**Vecina:**

El saludo más rolo que existe — neutro pero con mil significados según el tono. Tú lo usas y ya estás hablando como un capitalino de pura cepa.

**Meaning:**

Neutral Bogotá greeting meaning "how's it?"

**Example:**

¿Qué tal? No me diga que otra vez llovió en el momento equivocado.

**Translation:**

How's it? Don't tell me it rained at the worst moment again.

---

**Entry 8**

**¿Bien o qué?**

**Vecina:**

Seco, directo, con ese humor rolo que no sonríe mucho. Tú lo dices y la gente entiende que estás chequeando sin invadir.

**Meaning:**

Quick check meaning "good or what?"

**Example:**

¿Bien o qué? Porque la cara dice otra cosa.

**Translation:**

Good or what? Because your face is saying something else.

---

**Entry 9**

**¿Cómo está la vaina?**

**Vecina:**

"La vaina" es la palabra rola por excelencia — todo es una vaina. Tú la usas y ya estás dentro del juego bogotano sin tener que dar explicaciones largas.

**Meaning:**

Casual Bogotá greeting meaning "how's the thing / situation?"

**Example:**

¿Cómo está la vaina? ¿Ya arregló ese problema o sigue igual?

**Translation:**

How's the thing? Did you fix that problem or is it still the same?

---

**Entry 10**

**¿Todo bajo control?**

**Vecina:**

Ironía pura — en Bogotá nada está bajo control, pero igual preguntamos. Tú lo sueltas y la gente te responde con una sonrisa medio sarcástica.

**Meaning:**

Ironic check meaning "everything under control?"

**Example:**

¿Todo bajo control? Porque el tráfico dice que no.

**Translation:**

Everything under control? Because the traffic says no.

---

---

# Aprobación con Clase Bogotana

Approval with Bogotá Class

(Entries 11–20)

---

**Entry 11**

**De una**

**Vecina:**

Tú dices "de una" y ya estás dentro — sin vueltas, sin pensarlo dos veces, puro estilo rolo eficiente que no pierde el tiempo.

**Meaning:**

Right away / instantly, no hesitation

**Example:**

¿Vamos? De una, no hay tiempo pa' cuentos.

**Translation:**

We going? Right away — no time for stories.

---

**Entry 12**

**Eso está chévere**

**Vecina:**

"Chévere" pero sin exagerar — tú lo usas y suenas rolo de verdad, aprobando con clase y sin armar escándalo.

**Meaning:**

That's cool / nice (understated approval)

**Example:**

El plan está chévere, pero no me emocione mucho.

**Translation:**

The plan is cool — but don't get me too excited.

---

**Entry 13**

**Hágale**

**Vecina:**

Simple, directo, sin adornos — tú lo sueltas y ya estás dando el empujón rolo que dice "adelante, total qué perdemos".

**Meaning:**

Go for it / do it

**Example:**

¿Lo hacemos? Hágale, total qué perdemos.

**Translation:**

We doing it? Go for it — what do we have to lose?

---

**Entry 14**

**Eso quedó bien**

**Vecina:**

Bien hecho, sin alharaca, pero se nota — tú lo dices y la gente sabe que estás aprobando con ese toque elegante bogotano.

**Meaning:**

That turned out well / nicely done

**Example:**

El trabajo quedó bien, no hay queja.

**Translation:**

The work turned out well — no complaints.

---

**Entry 15**

**Me parece**

**Vecina:**

La aprobación rola clásica — no dice "sí" fuerte, pero tampoco "no". Tú lo usas y ya estás dando luz verde con clase.

**Meaning:**

Sounds good to me / I agree

**Example:**

¿Lo hacemos así? Me parece, dale.

**Translation:**

We do it like this? Sounds good to me — go ahead.

---

**Entry 16**

**Está perfecto**

**Vecina:**

"Perfecto" pero con ese toque irónico rolo que a veces es sarcasmo puro — tú lo dices y la gente capta el doble sentido al instante.

**Meaning:**

That's perfect (sometimes sarcastic)

**Example:**

Llegó tarde... está perfecto, como siempre.

**Translation:**

He arrived late... perfect, as usual.

---

**Entry 17**

**Va bien**

**Vecina:**

Va bien, sin euforia, pero aprobando — tú lo sueltas y suenas rolo eficiente que valora las cosas sin armar teatro.

**Meaning:**

It's going well / looking good

**Example:**

El proyecto va bien, no hay drama por ahora.

**Translation:**

The project is going well — no drama for now.

---

**Entry 18**

**Eso sí sirve**

**Vecina:**

Aprobación práctica y directa — si sirve, sirve. Punto. Tú lo dices y ya estás siendo el rolo útil que no pierde el tiempo.

**Meaning:**

That actually works / useful

**Example:**

Esa idea sí sirve, hay que probarla.

**Translation:**

That idea actually works — we should try it.

---

**Entry 19**

**Me cuadra**

**Vecina:**

"Me cuadra" es cuando algo encaja perfecto sin escándalo — tú lo usas y la gente sabe que estás aprobando con ese sentido práctico bogotano.

**Meaning:**

It fits / I like it / it works for me

**Example:**

El horario me cuadra, dale que sí.

**Translation:**

The schedule works for me — let's do it.

---

**Entry 20**
**Está al pelo**
**Vecina:**
Al pelo, perfecto, sin falla — tú lo dices y ya estás dando la aprobación rola más precisa, como si todo estuviera cuadrado.
**Meaning:**
Just right / spot on
**Example:**
El café está al pelo, ni muy caliente ni frío.
**Translation:**
The coffee is just right — not too hot, not cold.

---

## Emoción Contenida pero Real

Held-Back Emotions That Are Real

(Entries 21–30)

---

**Entry 21**

**Estoy que exploto**

**Vecina:**

When the excitement is too much to contain but you're still trying to play it cool, "estoy que exploto" is the rolo way to say it — you'll drop this and everyone will understand without you making a scene.

**Meaning:**

I'm about to burst / exploding with excitement

**Example:**

Estoy que exploto con esta noticia, ¡no lo puedo creer!

**Translation:**

I'm bursting with this news — I can't believe it!

---

**Entry 22**

**Me tiene contento**

**Vecina:**

When something has you quietly pleased, "me tiene contento" is the understated rolo way to admit it — you'll say it with a slight nod and people will know you're satisfied.

**Meaning:**

It's got me happy / pleased

**Example:**

El resultado me tiene contento, pero no canto victoria todavía.

**Translation:**

The result has me happy — but I'm not celebrating yet.

---

**Entry 23**

**Estoy motivado**

**Vecina:** When you're driven but keeping it under control, "estoy motivado" is how we say it in Bogotá — you'll use this and sound focused without sounding overly enthusiastic.

**Meaning:**

I'm motivated / driven

**Example:**

Estoy motivado para el proyecto, pero tranqui.

**Translation:**

I'm motivated for the project — but chill.

---

**Entry 24**

**Me voló la cabeza**

**Vecina:**

When something surprises you hard but you're still playing it cool, "me voló la cabeza" is the dry way we admit it blew our minds.

**Meaning:**

That blew my mind

**Example:**

El precio me voló la cabeza, pero qué berraquera de calidad.

**Translation:**

The price blew my mind — but what awesome quality.

---

**Entry 25**

**Estoy en mi salsa**

**Vecina:**

When you're right in your element and everything feels natural, "estoy en mi salsa" is the rolo way to say you're in your zone — understated but true.

**Meaning:**

I'm in my element / in my zone

**Example:**

Cuando hablo de Bogotá estoy en mi salsa.

**Translation:**

When I talk about Bogotá I'm in my element.

---

**Entry 26**

**Me tiene prendido**

**Vecina:**

When something has you energized but you're still keeping it controlled, "me tiene prendido" is how we say we're fired up without shouting it from the rooftops.

**Meaning:**

It's got me fired up / energized

**Example:**

El partido me tiene prendido, pero no grito.

**Translation:**

The game has me fired up — but I'm not yelling.

---

**Entry 27**

**Estoy que me subo**

**Vecina:**

When the energy is rising and you're starting to feel it, "estoy que me subo" is the rolo way to admit you're getting hyped — still calm on the outside.

**Meaning:**

I'm getting hyped / rising energy

**Example:**

Con esta música estoy que me subo, pero tranqui.

**Translation:**

With this music I'm getting hyped — but chill.

---

**Entry 28**

**Me dejó frío**

**Vecina:**

When something shocks you but you keep a straight face, "me dejó frío" is the classic rolo way to say it left you cold — understated impact.

**Meaning:**

That left me cold / shocked (understated)

**Example:**

La noticia me dejó frío, pero qué vaina.

**Translation:**

The news left me cold — what a thing.

---

**Entry 29**

**Estoy listo**

**Vecina:**

When you're prepared and ready without making a fuss, "estoy listo" is the straightforward rolo way to say you're set — no drama, just facts.

**Meaning:**

I'm ready / set

**Example:**

Estoy listo pa' lo que venga, dale.

**Translation:**

I'm ready for whatever comes — let's go.

---

**Entry 30**
**Me tiene pensando**
**Vecina:**
When something has you reflecting deeply but you're not showing it, "me tiene pensando" is how we say it's got us thinking hard — pure Bogotá style.
**Meaning:**
It's got me thinking hard
**Example:**
Esa propuesta me tiene pensando toda la noche.
**Translation:**
That proposal has me thinking all night.

---

## Rumba Bogotana que se Prende Despacio

Bogotá Rumba That Slowly Catches Fire
(Entries 31–40)

---

**Entry 31**

**Se armó el parche**

**Vecina:**

When the friends finally get together and the plan starts moving, "se armó el parche" is the dry rolo way to say the hangout is officially on — no big announcement, just facts.

**Meaning:**

The hangout / crew got together

**Example:**

Se armó el parche en Chapinero, tranqui pero bueno.

**Translation:**

The hangout got going in Chapinero — chill but good.

---

**Entry 32**

**Esto está chévere**

**Vecina:**

When the night is decent but you're not going to lose your head over it, "esto está chévere" is the understated rolo approval — you'll say it with a slight nod.

**Meaning:**

This is cool / nice party vibe

**Example:**

La rumba está chévere, pero no me emocione mucho.

**Translation:**

The party is cool — but don't get me too excited.

---

**Entry 33**

**Se prendió la cosa**

**Vecina:**

When the vibe finally starts to warm up, "se prendió la cosa" is how we say things are getting going — still controlled, never chaotic.

**Meaning:**

The thing got going / lit up

**Example:**

Llegó la música y se prendió la cosa.

**Translation:**

The music arrived and things got going.

---

**Entry 34**

**Esto está movido**

**Vecina:**

When the place has energy but you can still hold a conversation, “esto está movido” is the rolo way to say it’s lively without being overwhelming.

**Meaning:**

This is active / lively

**Example:**

El bar está movido, pero se puede hablar.

**Translation:**

The bar is lively — but you can still talk.

---

**Entry 35**

**Se armó la rumba**

**Vecina:**

When the party quietly kicks off, “se armó la rumba” is the classic rolo announcement no screaming, just a dry observation that the night has begun.

**Meaning:**

The party kicked off

**Example:**

Se armó la rumba en la 85, qué vaina tan buena.

**Translation:**

The party kicked off on 85th — what a nice thing.

---

**Entry 36**

**Esto está bueno**

**Vecina:**

When the atmosphere is solid but you're not going to lose your cool, "esto está bueno" is the restrained rolo way to say it's enjoyable.

**Meaning:**

This is good / enjoyable

**Example:**

El ambiente está bueno, pero no me voy a volver loco.

**Translation:**

The vibe is good — but I'm not going crazy.

---

**Entry 37**

**La cosa se puso intensa**

**Vecina:**

When the night gets a little heavier but you're still playing it cool, "la cosa se puso intensa" is how we acknowledge the shift — dry and observant.

**Meaning:**

The situation got intense

**Example:**

La cosa se puso intensa cuando empezó el reguetón.

**Translation:**

Things got intense when the reggaetón started.

---

**Entry 38**

**Esto está a otro nivel**

**Vecina:**

When the party quietly reaches the next level, "esto está a otro nivel" is the rolo way to say it's major league now — said with a raised eyebrow.

**Meaning:**

This is next level / major league now

**Example:**

Con este DJ esto está a otro nivel, qué berraquera.

**Translation:**

With this DJ this is next level — what a thrill.

---

**Entry 39**

**Aquí es la cosa**

**Vecina:**

When you've found the exact right spot, "aquí es la cosa" is the dry rolo way to say this is where it's happening — no hype, just truth.

**Meaning:**

This is the spot / where it's happening

**Example:**

Aquí es la cosa, el mejor parche de Bogotá.

**Translation:**

This is the spot — Bogotá's best hangout.

---

**Entry 40**

**Esto está lleno**

**Vecina:**

When the place is packed but you're still going in anyway, "esto está lleno" is the classic rolo complaint that somehow turns into acceptance.

**Meaning:**

This is packed / full

**Example:**

El bar está lleno, pero igual nos metemos.

**Translation:** The bar is packed — but we're going in anyway.

---

## Plata y la Realidad Capitalina

Money and Capital Reality

(Entries 41–50)

**Entry 41**

**Estoy en la olla**

**Vecina:**

When your wallet is officially empty and you're surviving on hope, "estoy en la olla" is the dry rolo way to say you're broke — you'll drop this at the end of the month and every capitalino will nod in solidarity.

**Meaning:**

I'm broke / in the pot

**Example:**

Estoy en la olla, ni pa'l TransMilenio tengo.

**Translation:**

I'm broke — not even enough for TransMilenio.

**Entry 42**

**No tengo ni pa'l bus**

**Vecina:**

Zero pesos, not even bus fare — you say this with a straight face and people know exactly how it feels in Bogotá at the end of the month.

**Meaning:**

Don't even have for the bus / zero money

**Example:**

No tengo ni pa'l bus, qué vaina tan salada.

**Translation:**

Not even enough for the bus — what bad luck.

---

**Entry 43**

**Quedé limpio**

**Vecina:**

After spending everything, "quedé limpio" is the rolo way to say you're left with nothing — said with quiet dignity, as if it's just another Tuesday.

**Meaning:**

Left clean / with nothing

**Example:**

Después de la salida quedé limpio, pero valió la pena.

**Translation:**

After going out I was left with nothing — but it was worth it.

---

**Entry 44**

**Estoy pelado**

**Vecina:**

"Pelado" means broke but still standing — you'll use this and your friends will laugh because they're probably in the same boat right now.

**Meaning:**

I'm broke / skinned

**Example:**

Estoy pelado, pero igual invito un tinto.

**Translation:**

I'm broke — but I'll still buy a coffee.

---

**Entry 45**

**No hay con qué**

**Vecina:**

When there's literally no money to do anything, "no hay con qué" is the straightforward rolo way to say everything is on hold — no drama, just reality.

**Meaning:**

There's nothing to work with / no funds

**Example:**

No hay con qué salir, toca quedarse en casa.

**Translation:**

No money to go out — gotta stay home.

---

**Entry 46**

**Estoy sin blanca**

**Vecina:**

Classic rolo expression for being completely broke — you say it with a shrug and everyone understands the capital struggle.

**Meaning:**

I'm without a dime / broke

**Example:**

Estoy sin blanca, pero la vida sigue.

**Translation:**

I'm without a dime — but life goes on.

---

**Entry 47**

**La plata se me fue volando**

**Vecina:**

When the money disappears faster than expected, "la plata se me fue volando" is the dry way we say it flew away — you'll hear this every payday in Bogotá.

**Meaning:**

The money disappeared super fast

**Example:**

La plata se me fue volando en tres días, qué berraquera de salado.

**Translation:**

The money flew away in three days — what terrible luck.

---

**Entry 48**

**Ando seco**

**Vecina:**

When your pockets are bone-dry, "ando seco" is the simple rolo way to say you're out of cash — said without self-pity, just stating the facts.

**Meaning:**

I'm dry / no money

**Example:**

Ando seco, pero igual me visto bien.

**Translation:**

I'm dry — but I still dress well.

---

**Entry 49**

**No tengo ni pa'l pasaje**

**Vecina:**

When you don't even have fare for the bus, "no tengo ni pa'l pasaje" is the honest capital way to say you're stuck — you'll use this and people will sympathize immediately.

**Meaning:**

Don't even have for the fare / no money at all

**Example:**

No tengo ni pa'l pasaje, toca caminar.

**Translation:**

Not even enough for the fare — gotta walk.

---

**Entry 50**

**Estoy quebrado**

**Vecina:**

When you're financially broken for the moment but tomorrow might be better, "estoy quebrado" is the rolo way to say it — dry, realistic, and quietly hopeful.

**Meaning:**

I'm broken / financially ruined

**Example:**

Estoy quebrado, pero mañana llega la plata.

**Translation:**

I'm broke — but the money arrives tomorrow.

---

## Carácter Rolo de Verdad

Real Rolo Character
(Entries 51–60)

**Entry 51**

**Ese man es una fiera**

**Vecina:**

When someone is tough and doesn't let anyone push him around, "ese man es una fiera" is the rolo way to say he's a beast — you'll say it with a slight nod and everyone will know exactly what you mean.

**Meaning:**

That guy is a beast / tough as hell

**Example:**

Ese man es una fiera negociando, no le bajan el precio.

**Translation:**

That guy is a beast at negotiating — they can't lower his price.

**Entry 52**

**No se le arruga a nadie**

**Vecina:**

This is the highest compliment we give someone who never flinches — you'll drop this line and people will instantly respect the person you're describing, puro carácter capitalino.

**Meaning:**

Doesn't back down from anyone / fearless

**Example:**

Ese parce no se le arruga a nadie, siempre responde.

**Translation:**

That partner doesn't back down from anyone — always steps up.

---

**Entry 53**

**Tiene calle ese man**

**Vecina:**

When someone really knows how Bogotá works, "tiene calle" is our way of saying he's got real street smarts — you'll sound like a true rolo when you use it.

**Meaning:**

That guy has street smarts / real-world experience

**Example:**

Tiene calle ese man, sabe cómo manejarse en cualquier lado.

**Translation:**

That guy has street smarts — knows how to handle himself anywhere.

---

**Entry 54**
**Se para firme donde sea**
**Vecina:**
When someone stands their ground no matter the situation, "se para firme donde sea" is how we say he doesn't flinch — said with quiet respect, typical Bogotá style.
**Meaning:**
Stands firm anywhere / doesn't flinch
**Example:**
Se para firme donde sea, no le tiembla la voz.
**Translation:**
He stands firm anywhere — his voice never shakes.

---

**Entry 55**
**Es de los que no copia**
**Vecina:**
When someone has their own style and never copies anyone, "es de los que no copia" is the elegant way we praise originality — you'll use this and people will nod in agreement.
**Meaning:**

Doesn't copy others / has his own original style

**Example:**

Es de los que no copia, siempre tiene su flow propio.

**Translation:**

He's one who doesn't copy — always has his own flow.

---

**Entry 56**

**No come de cuento**

**Vecina:**

This is for the sharp ones who never fall for nonsense — you say it and everyone knows the person stays alert, puro pilas rolo.

**Meaning:**

Doesn't fall for bs / stays alert

**Example:**

Ese no come de cuento, siempre está pilas con todo.

**Translation:**

He doesn't fall for nonsense — always stays sharp.

---

**Entry 57**

**Tiene más mundo que muchos**

**Vecina:**

When someone has seen and lived more than most, "tiene más mundo que muchos" is how we say they're way more experienced — said with that understated Bogotá respect.

**Meaning:**

Has seen more of the world / way more experienced

**Example:**

Tiene más mundo que muchos, sabe cómo es la cosa.

**Translation:**

He's seen more of the world than most — he knows how it works.

**Entry 58**

**No le baja la mirada a nadie**

**Vecina:**

This is pure confidence — when someone never lowers their gaze, you say this and every rolo understands they're solid and fearless.

**Meaning:**

Doesn't lower his gaze to anyone / confident as hell

**Example:**

No le baja la mirada a nadie, siempre firme.

**Translation:**

He doesn't lower his gaze to anyone — always solid.

**Entry 59 Es de los que responde duro Vecina:**

When someone steps up strong when it matters, "es de los

que responde duro" is the way we praise them — said with quiet admiration, puro carácter capitalino.

**Meaning:**

Steps up hard when needed / delivers strongly

**Example:**

Es de los que responde duro cuando la cosa se pone fea.

**Translation:**

He's one who steps up hard when things get tough.

---

**Entry 60**

**No se deja montar**

**Vecina:**

This is for the ones who never let anyone push them around — you say it and every rolo knows they set their own boundaries with class and without raising their voice.

**Meaning:**

Doesn't let anyone push him around

**Example:**

Ese man no se deja montar, siempre pone los puntos.

**Translation:**

That guy doesn't let anyone push him around — always sets boundaries.

---

## Estado Mental y la Vaina de la Mente

Mood and the Whole Mind Thing

(Entries 61–70)

**Entry 61**

**Estoy fundido**

**Vecina:**

When the city has drained every last bit of energy, "estoy fundido" is the rolo way to say you're burnt out — you'll use this after a long TransMilenio ride and everyone will understand without you explaining.

**Meaning:**

I'm burned out / no battery left

**Example:**

Después de la rumba estoy fundido, modo avión.

**Translation:**

After the party I'm burned out — airplane mode.

**Entry 62**

**Quedé hecho nada**

**Vecina:**

When the traffic or the week leaves you completely exhausted, "quedé hecho nada" is the dry rolo way to say you're wiped out — said with quiet resignation, as if it's just another Tuesday.

**Meaning:**

Left as nothing / totally exhausted

**Example:**

El tráfico me dejó hecho nada, qué vaina.

**Translation:** The traffic left me exhausted — what a thing.

---

**Entry 63**

**No doy más**

**Vecina:**

When you've reached your absolute limit and can't go any further, "no doy más" is how we admit we're done — you'll say it with a sigh and people will nod without asking questions.

**Meaning:**

I can't go on / at my limit

**Example:**

No doy más, esta semana fue muy pesada.

**Translation:**

I can't go on — this week was too heavy.

---

**Entry 64**

**Estoy apagado**

**Vecina:**

When you're running on low energy and just want to be left alone, "estoy apagado" is the rolo way to say you're turned off — like putting yourself in airplane mode.

**Meaning:**

I'm turned off / low energy

**Example:**

Estoy apagado, el frío me mató.

**Translation:**

I'm turned off — the cold killed me.

---

**Entry 65**

**Ando bajoneado**

**Vecina:**

When your mood is low but you're still functioning, "ando bajoneado" is the understated rolo way to say you're feeling down — you'll use this and friends will know exactly what you mean.

**Meaning:**

I'm feeling down / bummed

**Example:**

Ando bajoneado por el trabajo, pero pasa.

**Translation:**

I'm feeling down about work — but it passes.

**Entry 66**

**Estoy en modo avión**

**Vecina:**

When you need to disconnect from everything, "estoy en modo avión" is the modern rolo way to say you're unavailable — you'll say it and people will leave you in peace.

**Meaning:**

I'm in airplane mode / disconnected

**Example:**

Estoy en modo avión, no quiero saber de nadie.

**Translation:**

I'm in airplane mode — don't want to hear from anyone.

---

**Entry 67**

**Todo está tranqui**

**Vecina:**

When there's no drama and life feels calm, "todo está tranqui" is the relaxed rolo way to say everything is cool — you'll use this and sound like you have it together.

**Meaning:**

Everything is calm / chill

**Example:**

Todo está tranqui, no hay que preocuparse.

**Translation:**

Everything is calm — no need to worry.

---

**Entry 68**

**Estoy relajado**

**Vecina:**

When you're truly at ease and the day feels manageable, "estoy relajado" is the simple rolo way to say you're chill — said while having a tinto and watching the rain.

**Meaning:**

I'm relaxed / chill

**Example:**

Estoy relajado tomando un tinto en la plaza.

**Translation:**

I'm relaxed — having a coffee in the plaza.

---

**Entry 69**

**La cabeza me da vueltas**

**Vecina:**

When too much is happening and your mind is spinning, "la cabeza me da vueltas" is how we say we're overwhelmed — you'll use this and people will sympathize without making a fuss.

**Meaning:**

My head is spinning / overwhelmed

**Example:**

Con tanto tráfico la cabeza me da vueltas.

**Translation:**

With all this traffic my head is spinning.

---

**Entry 70**

**Estoy en mi mundo**

**Vecina:**

When you're in your own head and don't want to be disturbed, "estoy en mi mundo" is the classic rolo way to say you're zoned out — you'll say it with headphones in and people will leave you alone.

**Meaning:**

I'm in my own world

**Example:**

Estoy en mi mundo con los audífonos, no me hablen.

**Translation:**

I'm in my own world with headphones — don't talk to me.

---

---

# Cultura Capitalina sin Vueltas

Capital Culture Without the Fluff
(Entries 71–80)

---

**Entry 71**

**Eso es pura vaina**

**Vecina:**

When something is just nonsense or overcomplicated, "eso es pura vaina" is the dry rolo way to dismiss it — you'll say it with a shrug and everyone will know you're not buying the story.

**Meaning:**

That's pure thing / nonsense / situation

**Example:**

Eso es pura vaina, no le dé tanta importancia.

**Translation:**

That's pure nonsense — don't give it so much importance.

---

**Entry 72**

**Qué berraquera**

**Vecina:**

When something is genuinely impressive, "qué berraquera" is the understated rolo way to say "what a thrill" — you'll drop this and sound like a true capitalino without sounding overly excited.

**Meaning:**

What a thrill / awesome

**Example:**

Qué berraquera de paisaje en Monserrate.

**Translation:**

What an awesome view from Monserrate.

---

**Entry 73**

**Así es Bogotá**

**Vecina:**

When the rain hits at the worst moment or the traffic is ridiculous, "así es Bogotá" is how we accept the chaos — you'll say it with a half-smile and every rolo will nod in recognition.

**Meaning:**

That's Bogotá for you

**Example:**

Así es Bogotá: llueve cuando menos lo esperas.

**Translation:**

That's Bogotá for you — it rains when you least expect it.

---

**Entry 74**

**No hay de otra**

**Vecina:**

When there's simply no other way, "no hay de otra" is the practical rolo way to say "that's how it is" — you'll use this and people will respect your realism.

**Meaning:**

There's no other way / that's how it is

**Example:**

No hay de otra, toca madrugar pa' llegar temprano.

**Translation:**

There's no other way — gotta wake up early to arrive on time.

---

**Entry 75**

**Qué salado**

**Vecina:**

When bad luck strikes again, "qué salado" is the classic rolo way to say "what bad luck" — you'll say it with a sigh and everyone will sympathize without making a fuss.

**Meaning:**

What bad luck

**Example:**

Qué salado, se dañó el TransMilenio otra vez.

**Translation:**

What bad luck — TransMilenio broke down again.

---

**Entry 76**

**Ahí es donde duele**

**Vecina:**

When you hit the exact weak spot, “ahí es donde duele” is how we point it out — you’ll use this and people will feel the truth without you having to explain further.

**Meaning:**

That’s where it hurts / the weak spot

**Example:**

Ahí es donde duele, cuando suben el pasaje.

**Translation:**

That’s where it hurts — when they raise the fare.

---

**Entry 77**

**Esto es Bogotá**

**Vecina:**

When the city is raining, traffic is insane, and you’re still going out anyway, “esto es Bogotá” is the proud rolo way to sum it up — you’ll say it and sound like you belong here.

**Meaning:**

This is Bogotá

**Example:**

Esto es Bogotá: llueve, hay tráfico y igual salimos.

**Translation:**

This is Bogotá — it rains, there's traffic, and we still go out.

---

**Entry 78**

**La cosa está jodida**

**Vecina:**

When the situation is genuinely messed up, "la cosa está jodida" is the blunt rolo way to say it — you'll use this and people will know you're being real without panic.

**Meaning:**

The situation is messed up

**Example:**

La cosa está jodida con el paro, pero tranqui.

**Translation:**

The situation is messed up with the strike — but chill.

---

**Entry 79**

**Todo bien**

**Vecina:**

The most sarcastic rolo phrase of all — you say "todo bien" when it's clearly not, and everyone understands the irony without you having to explain.

**Meaning:**

Everything's fine (often sarcastic)

**Example:**

¿Cómo va? Todo bien... mentiras.

**Translation:**

How’s it going? Everything’s fine… lies.

---

**Entry 80**

**Aquí se vive sabroso**

**Vecina:**

Even with the cold and the chaos, “aquí se vive sabroso” is how we say life in Bogotá is still worth it — you’ll use this and sound like a true capitalino who knows how to enjoy the ride.

**Meaning:**

Here life is enjoyed (Bogotá style)

**Example:**

Aquí se vive sabroso, con su frío y su caos.

**Translation:**

Here life is enjoyed — with its cold and its chaos.

---

# Representative Glossary

(CS-03 – Rolo Flavor)

**Vaina**

**Vecina:**

Our all-purpose word for any situation, problem, or thing — you'll say "qué vaina" with a shrug and every rolo will know exactly what you mean without needing details.

**Meaning:**

Thing / stuff / situation

**Tranqui**

**Vecina:**

The classic rolo way to say "chill" or "relaxed" — you'll use this when things are calm but you still want to sound slightly sarcastic about it.

**Meaning:**

Chill / calm

**Chévere**

**Vecina:**

Our understated way of saying something is cool or nice — you'll drop this with a half-smile and sound like a true capitalino without getting too excited.

**Meaning:**

Cool / nice (understated)

**Berraquera**

**Vecina:**

When something is genuinely impressive, "qué berraquera" is the dry rolo way to say "what a thrill" — said with a raised eyebrow and zero hype.

**Meaning:**

What a thrill / awesome

**Salado**

**Vecina:**

When bad luck strikes again, "qué salado" is how we say "what bad luck" — you'll use this with a sigh and every rolo will sympathize without making a scene.

**Meaning:**

What bad luck

**Pilas**

**Vecina:**

Sharp, alert, on point — being "pilas" is highly valued in Bogotá because you have to stay awake to survive the traffic and the chaos.

**Meaning:**

Sharp / alert

**Modo avión**

**Vecina:**

When you need to disconnect from everything, "modo avión" is the modern rolo way to say you're unavailable — you'll say it with headphones in and people will leave you alone.

**Meaning:**

Airplane mode / disconnected

**Jodida**

**Vecina:**

When the situation is genuinely messed up, "la cosa está jodida" is the blunt rolo way to say it — you'll use this and people will know you're being real without panic.

**Meaning:**

Messed up / complicated

## Todo bien

**Vecina:**

The most sarcastic rolo phrase of all — you say “todo bien” when it’s clearly not, and everyone understands the irony without you having to explain.

**Meaning:**

Everything’s fine (often sarcastic)

## Rolo

**Vecina:**

What we call ourselves — dry, capital-city style with a touch of irony. You’ll use this and instantly sound like you belong to the city that never sleeps but always complains.

**Meaning:**

Bogotá person / capital-city style

---

---

# Discover the Collection

**The 8-Volume Series**

Here's the full collection so you can keep exploring every corner of Colombia — from the mountains to the coast, without the fluff:

CS-01 – Colombian Slang for Brave Foreigners (National)
CS-02 – Paisa Slang for Brave Foreigners
CS-03 – Rolo Slang for Brave Foreigners
CS-04 – Caleño Slang for Brave Foreigners
CS-05 – Cafetero Slang for Brave Foreigners
CS-06 – Costeño Slang for Brave Foreigners
CS-07 – Santandereano & Boyacense Slang for Brave Foreigners
CS-08 – Pacific Coast Slang for Brave Foreigners

---

Acknowledgements
Vecina:

Gracias a los rolos que me enseñaron a querer esta ciudad caótica pero inolvidable. Aquí llueve cuando menos lo esperas, el tráfico te pone a prueba y aun así uno se queda. Ustedes me mostraron que Bogotá no se explica, se vive. Sin vueltas.

---

www.ingramcontent.com/pod-product-compliance
Lightning Source LLC
LaVergne TN
LVHW011052110826
845149LV00015B/3464